Addison-Wesley's

C++ Backpack Reference Guide

Peter J. DePasquale
The College of New Jersey

Boston San Francisco New York
London Toronto Sydney Tokyo Singapore Madrid
Mexico City Munich Paris Cape Town Hong Kong Montreal

Publisher	Greg Tobin
Senior Acquisitions Editor	Michael Hirsch
Production Supervisor	Marilyn Lloyd
Marketing Manager	Michelle Brown
Proofreader	Holly McLean-Aldis
Cover Designer	Joyce Cosentino Wells
Prepress and Manufacturing	Caroline Fell
Cover image © 2004 Photodisc	

Access the latest information about Addison-Wesley titles from our World Wide Web site: http://www.aw-bc.com/computing

Many of the designations used by manufacturers and sellers to distinguish their products are claimed as trademarks. Where those designations appear in this book, and Addison-Wesley was aware of a trademark claim, the designations have been printed in initial caps or all caps.

The programs and applications presented in this book have been included for their instructional value. They have been tested with care, but are not guaranteed for any particular purpose. The publisher does not offer any warranties or representations, nor does it accept any liabilities with respect to the programs or applications.

ISBN 0-321-35013-8
1 2 3 4 5 6 7 8 9 10-CRW-08 07 06 05

Acknowledgments

I deeply appreciate the comments, thoughts, and guidance of several people in writing this guide. Both Bryce Liskovec and Lester Wolfgang (my students) were invaluable in the review and design of this guide. Their dedication to finding typos, checking the source code, and providing feedback on how they would use this guide has been invaluable. Thanks also to John Lewis (Villanova University) and Joseph Chase (Radford University) whose friendship and professional opinions I cherish deeply.

The staff at Addison-Wesley has again been the best that one could hope to work with. Michael Hirsch, my editor, has been an outstanding resource against whom I constantly throw ideas. He is also a very solid player of the fine game of poker. Patty Mahtani and Marilyn Lloyd kept the whole process on track, and worked diligently to ensure that the best possible end result was produced – no matter how many times we fiddled with the document file. Thank you one and all!

Dedication

I dedicate this work to Lisa Hawbecker who brightens each day I am fortunate to spend with her. She has supported this effort in countless ways and has my deepest gratitude.

Note

In summarizing the language, every attempt was made to be brief and on topic. It should be noted that this guide is targeted for first-year programming students who are using C++ as their programming language. Thus, not every subtlety, reserved word, or library is covered due to space considerations. This guide is not a substitute for a good textbook, but it is intended to be a quick reference when needed.

When portions of the syntax are optional, they are enclosed in brackets. In places where additional statements would be placed, such as the body of a function or a class, ellipses (…) have been substituted. Example:

```
class ExampleClass {
private:
    bool variable-name [ = initial-value-expression ];
    …
};
```

In this example, the bool reserved word is highlighted for the discussion of its syntax and functionality. The initial value can be set through the use of the optional additional syntax. Since it is optional in nature, it has been surrounded by braces ([ ]) to indicate that this portion is optional.

Due to space constraints, the following C++ reserved words were not included in the reserved word summaries (center material) from this book. For first-year programming students, these are features of the language that you are not likely to utilize. Refer to your compiler's documentation for information regarding the use and meaning of these reserved words.

asm	const_cast	Dynamic_cast
explicit	export	reinterpret_cast
static_cast	wchar_t	

Contents

Commonly Used C++ Header Files

C++ Fundamentals

C++ Escape Sequences

Escape Sequence	Meaning
\'	single quote
\"	double quote
\?	question mark
\\	Backslash
\a	alert (bell)
\b	Backspace
\f	Formfeed
\n	newline
\r	carriage return
\t	Tab
\v	vertical tab
\OOO to \OOO	Escape code specified in octal (where each "O" is an octal digit [0-7])
\xHH to \xHH	Escape code specified in hexadecimal (where each "H" is a hexidecimal digit [0–9, a–f, or A–F])

C++ Numeric Primitive Types

Type	Storage	Min/Max Value	Note
short	typically 2 bytes	Dependent on the size set by the compiler. See the <climits> header file for the exact size on your system.	The size of a short is guaranteed to be less than or equal to the size of an int.
int	typically 4 bytes	Dependent on the size set by the compiler. See the <climits> header file for the exact size on your system.	The size of an int is guaranteed to be less than or equal to the size of a long.

Type	Storage	Min/Max Value	Note
long	typically 4 bytes	Dependent on the size set by the compiler. See the \<climits\> header file for the exact size on your system.the compiler.	
float	typically 4 bytes	Dependent on the size set by the compiler. See the \<cfloat\> header file for the exact size on your system.the compiler.	The size of a float is guaranteed to be less than or equal to the size of a double.
double	typically 8 bytes	Dependent on the size set by the compiler. See the \<cfloat\> header file for the exact size on your system.the compiler.	

C++ Logical Operators

Operator	Description	Example	Result
!	logical NOT	! a	"true" if a is "false," "false" if a is "true"
&&	logical AND	a && b	"true" if a and b are both "true," "false" otherwise
||	logical OR	a || b	"true" if a or b or both are "true," "false" otherwise

C++ Equality and Relational Operators

Operator	Meaning
==	equal to
!=	not equal to
<	less than
<=	less than or equal to
>	greater than
>=	greater than or equal to

C++ Bitwise Operators

Operator	Description
~	bitwise NOT
&	bitwise AND
|	bitwise OR
^	bitwise XOR
<<	left shift
>>	right shift

C++ Widening / Narrowing Conversions

From	To (Widening)	To (Narrowing)
short	int, long, float, or double	n/a
int	long, float, or double	Short
long	float or double	int or short
float	double	long, int, or short
double	n/a	float, long, int, or short

C++ Reserved Literals

C++ contains two literal values, which are reserved for special meanings. The literal values "true" and "false" represent the only two possible states for a Boolean value (bool) or expression. These literal values are most often used in conjunction with equality operators or assignment statements. The "true" and "false" literals may not be used as identifier names.

Both C and pre-standard C++ used a zero (0) integer value to represent the "false" value. Any non-zero integer value would also suffice for the "true" value. Though it is possible to continue to use this style, good programming practice encourages the use of "true" and "false" when working with bools.

C++ Member Access Level Qualifiers

Modifier	Affect on Constants, Variables, Data Types, and Functions
public	Members are accessible from any other location in the program.
protected	Members are accessible from only within the defining class.
private	Members are accessible from only within the defining class and derived classes.

C++ Inheritance Access Level Qualifiers

Modifier	Affect on Class Inheritance
public	Parent class members declared as public are public in the child class. Protected members in the parent class are protected in the child class.
protected	Parent class members declared as public or protected become protected in the child class.
private	Parent class members declared as public or protected become private in the child class.

C++ Operator Precedence

In an expression, operators at a lower precedence level are evaluated before those at a higher level (first column). Operators at the same level are evaluated according to the specified association (fourth column).

Precedence Level	Operator	Operation	Associates
1	:	Resolution of scope	N/A
2	[]	array indexing	
	.	object member selection	
	->	pointer member selection	
	(*parameters*)	function invocation	L to R
	++	postfix increment	
	--	postfix decrement	

Precedence Level	Operator	Operation	Associates
2 (cont.)	++	prefix increment	N/A
	--	prefix decrement	
	typeid	obtains dynamic type information	
	sizeof	obtains size of variable /type	
	+	unary plus	
	-	unary minus	
	~	bitwise NOT	
	!	logical NOT	
	&	Address of variable	
	*	Dereferencing of pointer	
	new / new[ ]	object memory allocation	
	delete / delete[ ]	object memory deallocation	
	*_cast<*type*>	C++ style cast to specified type	
	(*type*)	cast to specified type (R to L assoc.)	
3	.*	pointer to member	L to R
	->*	dereference and pointer to member	
4	*	Multiplication	L to R
	/	division	
	%	remainder	
5	+	Addition	L to R
	-	subtraction	
6	<<	bitwise left shift / output	L to R
	>>	bitwise right shift / input	
7	<	less than	L to R
	<=	less than or equal to	
	>	greater than	
	>=	greater than or equal to	
8	==	Equal	L to R
	!=	not equal	
9	&	bitwise AND	L to R
10	^	bitwise XOR	L to R
11	|	bitwise OR	L to R
12	&&	boolean AND	L to R
13	||	boolean OR	L to R
14	?:	conditional operator	R to L

Precedence Level	Operator	Operation	Associates
15	=	Assignment	R to L
	+=	addition, then assignment	
	-=	subtraction, then assignment	
	*=	multiplication, then assignment	
	/=	division, then assignment	
	%=	remainder, then assignment	
	<<=	left shift, then assignment	
	>>=	right shift, then assignment	
	&=	bitwise AND, then assignment	
	&=	boolean AND, then assignment	
	^=	bitwise XOR, then assignment	
	^=	boolean XOR, then assignment	
	|=	bitwise OR, then assignment	
	|=	boolean OR, then assignment	
16	**throw**	throws an exception	R to L
17	,	Expression sequencing	L to R

Summary of Selected C++ Header Files

Header File	Functionality
<cassert>	Provides access to the assert function.
<cctype>	Supports testing character values (e.g. upper case, lower case).
<cfloat>	Defines min/max float point values.
<climits>	Defines min/max integer data values.
<cmath>	Defines various math functions (e.g. sin, cos, tan) and important math constant values (e.g. E, PI, LOG2E).
<cstdlib>	Provides memory allocation/deallocation, absolute value, character conversion and other functions.
<cstring>	Supports string and memory manipulations.
<iomanip>	Provides predefined input and output stream manipulators.
<iostream>	Defines the standard stream objects cin, cout, and cerr.
<istream>	Defines the istream, ostream, and ios classes.
<fstream>	Defines the ifstream, ofstream, and fstream classes.
<string>	Provides the string data type (specialized version of the basic_string class), supporting functions to manipulate strings, and overloaded operators to operate on strings.

C++ Reserved Words

auto (modifier)

Syntax
[**auto**] data-type *variable-name* [= *initial-value-expression*];

Description
The **auto** reserved word specifies that a variable is automatic. That is, that the variable has a scope limited to the block in which it is defined.

Example

```
int main ( ) {
    auto int alpha = 55;
    short beta = 22;

    cout << "alpha=" << alpha << " beta=" << beta;

    return 0;
}
```

Tips
* The **auto** reserved word is rarely used by programmers as the behavior that it creates is the default behavior of block-scoped objects.

See also
None.

bool (data type)

Syntax
[modifier] **bool** *variable-name* [= *initial-value-expression*];

Description
The reserved word bool is used to declare one or more variables of the boolean data type (containing a "true" or "false" value).

Examples

```
// Declares a boolean variable named found and sets its initial value to "true":
bool found = true;
```

```
// Declares two boolean variables, minFound and maxFound, and sets
// maxFound's initial value to "false":
bool minFound, maxFound = false;
```

Tips

- When declaring a **bool** variable, you can optionally set the initial value of the variable by following the **variable name** with an equals sign and the **initial value expression** (as shown in brackets in the syntax statement).

- Multiple **bool** variables can be declared in the same statement by following each **variable name** with a comma (see the second example).

- As a function variable, **bool**s should be initialized prior to use. If they are not, the variable will assume the value defined by the representation of its memory location. That is, the bits contained at the variable's true location in memory will be converted to a value of the variable's type (e.g. a **bool**). Note that in this situation your compiler may provide a compile-time warning that the variable (when used) had not been initialized.

- **Bool**s can be cast to other data types, including shorts, ints, and longs.

- The intial value of a boolean variable can be an integer or floating point value (which may cause truncation). The value zero is generally considered to be the same as the value "false" and all other values are considered to be the same as the value "true".

See also

- false (p. 9)
- true (p. 9)

break (control)

Syntax
break;

Description
The **break** statement stops execution of the enclosing switch, while, do, or for loop (known as the **break** target) and continues execution following the enclosing statement.

Examples

```
// A switch statement involving an integer age variable.  The break
// statement prevents the execution path from falling into the next case.
```

```
switch (age) {
    case 16:
        cout << "Of legal driving age.";
        break;

    case 18:
        cout << "Of legal voting age.";
        break;
}
```

```
// Search the grades listing (array of integer student grades) for the first
// occurrence of a value of 100. If the target is found, the search terminates
// abruptly. Regardless of the search result, a boolean flag is set indicating
// the search result.
for (int index = 0; index < numItems; index ++) {
    if (grades[index] == 100) {
        found = true;
        break;
    } else
        found = false;
}
```

Tips

- If a **break** statement is not enclosed by a switch, while, do, or for loop, a compilation error will occur.
- The use of a **break** statement (except when used in conjunction with a switch statement) is considered a poor programming practice.
- If the **break** statement is absent from the end of a case clause, execution will continue through the next **case** label and its statements (if present).

See also

- case (p. 15)
- do (p. 25)
- for (p. 30)
- switch (p. 52)
- while (p. 67)

case (control)

Syntax

```
switch ( expression ) {
    // One or more case clauses of the form
    [ case constant-expression:
        statement(s);
```

```
        [ break; ]
    ]

    [ default:
        statement(s);
        [ break; ]
    ]
}
```

Description

The **case** label is used within switch statements to define executable blocks of code to be executed when the switch's expression evaluates to the **case** label's **constant expression**.

Examples

```
char letter = 'i';
string characterType = "unknown";

// Switch on the letter variable.
switch (letter) {
    // if 'letter' is 'a', 'e', 'i', 'o', or 'u' set the type to "vowel"
    case 'a':
    case 'e':
    case 'i':
    case 'o':
    case 'u':
        characterType = "vowel";
        break;

    // Otherwise, set the type to consonant.
    default:
        characterType = "consonant";
        break;
}
```

```
int value = 3;

// Switch on the value variable.
switch (value) {
    // If value is 1, increment by one.
    case 1:
        value++;
        break;
```

```
// If value is 3, increment by two.
case 3:
    value += 2;
    break;
}
```

Tips
- The **constant expression** must be a bool, char, short, or integer literal.
- **Constant expressions** within the same switch statement must be unique. One or more statements, terminated with a break statement, generally follow **case** labels. If the break statement is absent, execution will continue through the next **case** label and its statements (if present); **case** labels can also cascade through this mechanism, as shown in the first example.
- The default label can be used to define a block of statements (like a **case** label) that are executed if no **case** label matches the constant expression.

See also
- break (p. 14)
- default (p. 23)
- switch (p. 52)

catch (control)

Syntax
```
try {
    statement(s);
}
catch (data-type variable-name) {
    statement(s);
}
```

Description
The **catch** reserved word is part of the larger try/**catch** statement. Both of these reserved words enclose a block of one or more statements that are executed under certain circumstances. The try block is executed first, until it completes execution of its statements or an exception is thrown.

If an exception arises, each **catch** clause is examined one at a time, in linear order, to determine whether the thrown exception matches a particular **exception type**. A match is made if the type of the exception thrown can be assigned to the type being caught. If a match does occur, the statement(s) in the matching **catch** clause are executed. If an exception does not arise while executing the try block, processing will continue following the last **catch** block.

Examples

```
// This function calculates the inverse of the specified int if the value
// passed is greater than zero.  Otherwise, it throws an exception.
double inverse (int denominator) {
    double result = 0;
    try {
        if (denominator <= 0) {
            string errString = "The denominator must be greater than 0.";
            throw errString;
        } else
            result = 1.0 / denominator;
    }
    catch (string err) {
        cout << err;
    }
    return result;
}
```

```
// This function provides a simple example of throwing (and catching) an
// integer value.
void one ( ) {
    int x = 5;
    try {
        if (x==5)
            // Throw an integer value as an exception
            throw 5;
    }

    // Integer values can also be thrown/caught
    catch (int numErr) {
        cout<< "Caught error number: " << numErr << endl;
    }

    // Catch any type of exception
    catch (...) {
        cout << "Catch-all triggered.  Exception caught." << endl;
    }
}
```

Tips

- The type of exception caught by a **catch** expression may be a pointer to an object.
- You can catch any type of exception thrown by placing an ellipsis as the formal parameter to a **catch** block. See the second example above.
- A try block must be followed by one or more **catch** blocks associated with it, as long as a different type of exception is being caught by each clause.
- Generally, programmers use the **catch** clause to correct a potential error and proceed with processing. Some programmers use a **catch** clause to print a warning message or a trace of the program. In the event of a critical issue, it is possible to terminate the program abruptly within a **catch** clause.

See also
- try (p. 57)

char (data type)

Syntax
[modifier] **char** *variable-name* [= *initial-value-expression*];

Description
The reserved word **char** is used to declare one or more variables of the **char** data type (which contains character data values).

Examples

```
// Declares a char variable named firstLetter and sets its initial value to 'p'.
char firstLetter = 'p';
```

```
// Declares two char variables, alpha and beta, and sets beta's initial value to '*'.
char alpha, beta = '*';
```

Tips

- When declaring a **char** variable, you can optionally set the initial value of the variable by following the variable name with an equals sign and the initial value expression (as shown in brackets in the syntax statement).
- Multiple **char** variables can be declared in the same statement by following each variable name with a comma (see the second example).
- A **char** variable should always be initialized prior to use. Failing to do so will likely result in a compile-time warning. In some cases, the data stored in the memory allocated to the character variable will be used as the initial value of the variable. This may lead to curious (seemingly random) initial values for the variable.

See also
None.

class (class–related)

Syntax

class *class-name* [: [*public*] *class-name-to-extend* [, *class-name-to-extend*]] {
   // Class members (variables and functions) are defined here.
};

or

template < **class** class-name [, typename/ **class** *data-type/class-name*] >
class *class-name* { ... }

or

template < **class** T>
return-type function-name ([*parameter-list*]){ ... }

Description

The **class** reserved word is used to define the implementation of a class in the C++ language. Classes can contain member variables (instance data) and functions (used to perform operations on the instance data and provide other supporting functionality).

Additionaly, you can use the **class** reserved word when defining a template's parameter list (see the second and third syntax examples above).

Example

```
// Defines a simple class to represent an address (of a building, house, etc.)
class Address {
private:
    int number;
    string street;
    string city;
    string state;
    int zip;

public:
    // The constructor for the Address class.
    Address (int num, string str, string cty, string st, int zipCode) {
        number = num;
        street = str;
        city = cty;
```

```
        state = st;
        zip = zipCode;
    }

    // Returns the zip code for this address
    int getZip ( ) {
        return zip;
    }

    // Sets the number of this address to the specified value.
    void setNumber (int newNumber) {
        number = newNumber;
    }
};
```

Tips
*   A **class** can inherit from one or more other **classes**—this is known as inheritance. Inheritance occurs by modifying the definition of a **class**.

See also
*   delete (p. 24)
*   new (p. 40)
*   template (p. 54)

const (modifier)

Syntax:
[**const**] *data-type variable-name* = *initial-value-expression;*
or
member-function [**const**];

Description:
The reserved word **const** is used to augment the definition of a variable or function. When used in conjunction with a variable's declaration, the **const** reserved word marks the variable as unable to be modified in the source code. That is, the initial value of the declared variable cannot be changed.

When used in conjunction with a function declaration, the **const** reserved word prohibits a function from attempting to modify a private data member's value (except those data members marked as mutable). If an executable statement within a **const** member function attempts to modify such a value, a compile time error results. Const member functions are also prohibited from calling other, non-const member functions.

Examples

```
// Define the age to always be 36 years old.
const int age = 36;
```

```
// Define the external variable height
const extern double height;
```

```
// Declare the calculate function to be a const member function
int calculate ( ) const;
```

Tip

- When **const** is used with the declaration of a variable, the variable must have an accompanying initialization, unless the variable is also marked as extern.

See also

- extern (p. 29)
- mutable (p. 38)

---

continue (control)

Syntax

continue;

Description

The **continue** statement terminates processing of the current iteration of a loop at the point of the statement. This behavior is similar to that of a break statement, but rather than terminating the loop completely, the **continue** statement evaluates the loop condition and iterates again through the loop if the condition yields a "true" value.

Example

```
while (alpha < 5) {
    // Increment alpha and terminate this iteration of the loop.
    alpha++;
    if (alpha > 0)
        continue;

    // The increment of beta is never executed.
    beta++;
}
```

Tips

- The **continue** statement can also be used in do and for loops.

- A compile-time error will occur if a **continue** statement is not enclosed by a do, for, or while loop.

- Care should be exercised when using the **continue** statement, as it may make source code more difficult to read.

See also
- do (p. 25)
- for (p. 30)
- true (p. 9)
- while (p. 67)

---

default (control)

Syntax
default:

Description
The **default** label is used within switch statements to define executable blocks of code to be executed in the event that the switch's expression fails to evaluate to any existing case label's constant expression.

Example

```
char letter = 'i';
string characterType = "unknown";

// Switch on the letter variable.
switch (letter) {
    // if 'letter' is 'a', 'e', 'i', 'o', or 'u' set the type to "vowel"
    case 'a':
    case 'e':
    case 'i':
    case 'o':
    case 'u':
        characterType = "vowel";
        break;

    // Otherwise, set the type to consonant.
    default:
        characterType = "consonant";
        break;
}
```

Tips

- A **default** label is not followed by a constant expression, unlike the case labels also present in switch statements.

- The **default** label is generally listed last in the switch statement block. This helps distinguish it from the case labels. However, if the default label appears earlier in the list of labels, it does not impede the ability to correctly match case labels found later in the switch statement block.

See also

- case (p. 15)

- switch (p. 52)

delete (operator)

Syntax

delete *pointer;*

or

delete [ ] *pointer;*

Description

The **delete** operator deallocates the memory associated with the object pointed to by the specified *pointer*.

Example

```
// Creates an automobile object with default values
// and then destroys it to recover the memory.
int main ( ) {
    Automobile* myCar = new Automobile;
    cout << "Number of wheels: " << myCar->getWheels ( );

    delete myCar;
    return 0;
}
```

Tips

- When **delete** is used to deallocate an object's memory, the object's destructor is called first (prior to deallocation) if the destructor is present.

- The **delete** operator has no effect when the operation is performed on the null pointer.

- You may also use the **delete** operator to delete memory allocated to an array. Use the second form of the **delete** operator (with the empty brackets preceding the pointer to the array) to do so.

See also
- new (p. 40)

---

do (control)

Syntax
do
>   *statement;*
while (*boolean-expression*);

Description
The **do** reserved word is used to construct a loop that executes the specified statement one or more times until the expression following the while reserved word evaluates to a "false" value.

Example

```
// Continually loop and increase the value of alpha until alpha's value exceeds 5.
do
    alpha += beta;
while (alpha < 5);
```

Tips
- The statement portion of the **do** loop always executes at least once.
- If the **boolean expression** does not resolve to a boolean result ("true" [non-zero value] or "false" [zero value]), a compile-time error is generated.
- To execute multiple statements as the body of the **do** loop, enclose the statements to execute in braces, creating a statement block.
- Be sure that the **boolean expression** changes as part of the body of the loop. If the value of the expression does not change, the loop will be performed endlessly. This situation is known as an *endless loop*.
- Keep in mind that the **boolean expression** can comprise multiple boolean expressions, each joined by logical operators.
- A **do** loop may contain other loops (**do**, for, while), thereby creating nested loops.
- Break and continue statements can be used in **do** loops.
- A common mistake is to forget to insert a semicolon (;) following the **boolean expression**.

See also

- break (p. 14)
- do (p. 25)
- for (p. 30)
- while (p. 67)

continue (p. 22)
false (p. 9)
true (p. 9)

.

double (data type)

Syntax

[modifier] **double** *variable-name* [= *initial-value-expression*];

Description

The reserved word **double** is used to declare one or more variables of the **double** data type.

Examples

```
// Declares a double variable named alpha and sets its initial value to 45.6964.
double alpha = 45.6964;
```

```
// Declares two double variables, beta and gamma, and sets gamma's initial
// value to -55.112.
double beta, gamma = -55.112;
```

Tips

- When declaring a **double** variable, you can optionally set the initial value of the variable by following the variable name with an equals sign and the initial value expression (as shown in brackets in the syntax statement).
- Multiple **double** variables can be declared in the same statement by following each variable name with a comma (see the second example).
- A **double** variable should always be initialized prior to use. Failing to do so will likely result in a compile-time warning. In some cases, the data stored in the memory allocated to the double **double** will be used as the initial value of the variable. This may lead to curious (seemingly random) initial values for the variable.

See also

None.

else (control)

Syntax

if (*boolean-expression*)

statement;
[**else**
    statement;
]

Description

The **else** reserved word is used to provide an alternative statement to execute in the event that an if statement's boolean expression resolves to "false". When used in conjunction with the if statement, a programmer can create an execution path for a "true" or "false" result in an if statement.

Examples

```
// Check to see whether the number of students in the course is equal to 25. If so,
// close this section. Otherwise, ensure that the section remains open.
if (numberOfStudents == 25)
    classFull = true;
else
    classFull = false;
```

```
// If the user-entered value is the string "C++", then print the names of two
// other OOP languages. Otherwise, print the names of two procedural languages.
if (enteredValue == "C++") {
    cout << "Smalltalk" << "\n";
    cout << "Java" << "\n";
} else {
    cout << "Pascal" << "\n";
    cout << "Fortran" << "\n";
}
```

Tips

- The **else** reserved word (and its corresponding statement) is an optional part of the if conditional statement.
- To execute multiple statements as part of the **else** clause of an if statement, enclose the statements to execute with braces, creating a statement block (see the second example).

See also

- false (p. 9)
- if (p. 34)

- true (p. 9)

enum (data type)

Syntax

[modifier] **enum** *data-type* { *value1, value2, value3, …* }

Description

The **enum** reserved word defines a new data type and corresponding values that the type may store. Identifiers created from this new data type can store only values listed in the data type's definition (*value1, value2, value3* in the syntax statement).

Example

```
// Define the Member data type and permit only the following values.
enum Member {Bono, Larry, Edge, Adam};

// Define the Team data type and provide specific default values
enum Team {Quarterback=12, WideOut=5, RunningBack=-45};

// Create specific identifiers for each band member and set their
// appropriate values based on each member's role in the band.
Member vocals = Bono;
Member bass = Adam;
Member drums = Larry;
Member lead = Edge;

// Print the values of the membership of the band through
// a variety of approaches.
cout << "Vocals: " << vocals << endl;
cout << "Drums: " << drums << endl;
cout << "Lead Guitar: " << lead << endl;
cout << "Bass Guitar: " << bass << endl;
```

Tips

- The values of an enumerated type are stored as integer values. The first identifier, by default, is stored as a zero (0) value, the second as a one (1), and so on.
- To assign specific values (rather than the default) to an enumerator, a simple initialization assignment can be placed in the enumerator's definition. (See the definition of the Team data type in the example above.)
- Attempting to assign an invalid value (other than one of the specified possible values) to an **enum** variable will produce a compile-time error.
- Only the value assigned to an enumerator is accessible. The name (e.g. "Bono" in the Member data type above) is inaccessible as the value of a variable. Thus, when

accessed as part of an expression (see the output expression(s) in the example above), the value 0 is printed as the value of the vocals variable.

See also
None.

extern (modifier)

Syntax
[**extern**] *data-type variable-name*;

Description
The **extern** reserved word specifies that declared variable (*variable-name*) is a global variable that is defined elsewhere (usually in another source code file).

Example

```
int main ( ) {
    // Obtain the versionNumber variable from another source or header file
    extern string versionNumber;

    // Print a simple welcome message using the versionNumber variable which was
    // declared and defined in a header file.
    cout << "Welcome to the C++ Backpack Reference Guide " << endl;
    cout << "version: " << versionNumber << endl;

    return 0;
}
```

Tips
• Global variables are generally considered poor programming practice and should be avoided. However, if you need to obtain access to an existing variable defined elsewhere; the **extern** declaration modifier can be used to declare the desired variable locally.

See also
None.

float (data type)

Syntax
[modifier] **float** *variable-name* [= *initial-value-expression*];

Description
The reserved word **float** is used to declare one or more variables of the **float** data type.

Examples

```
// Declares a float variable named alpha and
// sets its initial value to 6.965.
float alpha = 6.965f;
```

```
// Declares two float variables, beta and gamma, and
// sets gamma's initial value to -12.345F.
float beta, gamma = -12.345F;
```

Tips

- When declaring a **float** variable, you can optionally set the initial value of the variable by following the variable name with an equals sign and the initial value expression (as shown in brackets in the syntax statement).

- Multiple **float** variables can be declared in the same statement by following each variable name with a comma (see the second example).

- A **float** variable should always be initialized prior to use. Failing to do so will likely result in a compile-time warning. In some cases, the data stored in the memory allocated to the character variable will be used as the initial value of the variable. This may lead to curious (seemingly random) initial values for the variable.

- To reduce the confusion between doubles, **float**s, and other data types which store floating point data, it is customary to append either the 'f' or the 'F' character when specifying a literal **float** value. This often occurs when initializing **float** variables. (See the examples above.)

See also
None.

for (control)

Syntax
for (*initializer-expression*; *test-expression*; *update-expression*)
    statement;

Description

The **for** reserved word is used to construct a loop that executes the specified statement until the **test expression** evaluates to a "false" value. Before the first attempted execution of the loop, the **initializer expression** is executed (generally used to set loop control variables).

Next, the **test expression** is evaluated. If the **test expression** evaluates to a "true" result, the statement in the loop body is executed. Following each iteration of the loop, the **update expression** is performed, and then the **test expression** is reevaluated. If the test expression evaluates to a "false" result, the loop terminates and control passes to the statement following the loop.

The **initializer expression** may optionally declare a variable and set its initial value (see the examples). If declared in the **initializer expression**, the variable is accessible only in the body of the loop; it is not accessible outside the loop.

The **initializer expression_and **update expression** may contain several expressions separated by commas (see second example). The **test expression** can comprise multiple expressions joined by zero or more logical operators.

Examples

```
// This loop is controlled by alpha (decreasing from 5 to 1). Each time through the
// loop, the value of alpha is decremented and printed.
for (int alpha = 5; alpha > 0; alpha--)
    cout << "alpha's value is: " << alpha << endl;
```

```
// This loop is controlled by beta (decreasing from 5 to 1). Each time through
// the loop, beta decreases by one, gamma increases by one, and the values
// of beta and gamma are printed.
for (int beta = 5, gamma = 0; beta > 0; beta--, gamma++) {
    cout << "beta's value is: " << beta << endl;
    cout << "gamma's value is: " << gamma << endl;
}
```

Tips

- To execute multiple statements as the body of the **for** loop, enclose the statements to execute in braces, creating a statement block (see the second example).
- Be sure that the **boolean expression** eventually changes as part of the body of the loop. If the value of the expression never changes, the loop will be performed endlessly. This situation is known as an *endless loop*.
- A **for** loop may contain other loops (do, **for,** while), thereby creating *nested loops*.
- Break and continue statements can be used in **for** loops.

See also

- break (p. 14)
- continue (p. 22)

- do (p. 25)
- while (p. 67)

friend (class-related)

Syntax
friend class *class-name*;

or

friend *return-type function-name* ([*parameter-list*]);

Description
The **friend** reserved word is used to expose all private members of a class to another class or a specific function. By doing so, the named class or function can opening access or modify private data or execute private functions of the enclosing class.

Example

```
class BlackjackCard {
private:
    string face; // Stores the string name of the face, if this card is a face card
                 //  (e.g. "Ace", "King", etc.).  If this card is not a face card, then
                 //  the value stored is "Non-face".

    int value; // Stores the value of this card (1-11)
    char suit; // Stores a character representing the suit of this card (e.g. 'C'=clubs,
               //  'S'=spades, 'D'=diamonds, 'H'=hearts)
public:
    BlackjackCard (string face, int value, char suit) {
        this->face = face;
        this->value = value;
        this->suit = suit;
    }

    friend string getCardFace (const BlackjackCard& card);
    friend int getCardValue (const BlackjackCard& card);
    friend class CasinoCheater;
};

// A "friend" function which returns the face information about the specified card.
string getCardFace (const BlackjackCard& card) {
    return card.face;
}
```

```
class CasinoCheater {
public:
    // A sample function which is a "friend" of the BlackjackCard because it
    // is a member function of a "friend" class.
    void changeSuit (char newSuit, BlackjackCard& card) {
        card.suit = newSuit;
    }
};

// A "friend" function which returns the value of the specified card.
int getCardValue (const BlackjackCard& card) {
    return card.value;
}

int main ( ) {
    // Instantiate a BlackjackCard object and then print the
    // card's face and value.
    BlackjackCard bjc ("Ace", 11, 'D');
    cout << "Your card's face: " << getCardFace (bjc) << endl;
    cout << "Your card's value: " << getCardValue (bjc);

    return 0;
}
```

Tips
- **Friend**s of a class must be named within the definition of the class.
- **Friend**ship is not inherited.

See also
None.

goto (control)

Syntax
goto *label-name*;

Description
The **goto** statement transfers execution of a program from the point of the **goto** statement to the specified destination.

Example

```cpp
int main ( ) {
    int enteredValue = 0;  // Stores the value entered by the user

    // Prompt the user for an integer value
    cout << "Enter an integer number: ";
    cin >> enteredValue;

    if (enteredValue > 0)
        goto positive;
    else if (enteredValue < 0)
        goto negative;
    else {
        cout << "The value is zero!";
        goto end;
    }

positive:
    cout << "The value is positive.";
    goto end;

negative:
    cout << "The value is negative.";

end:
    cout << endl;
    return 0;
}
```

Tip

- **Goto** statements are widely considered to be a poor programming practice since they lead to code that is less structured and more difficult to read.

See also
None.

if (control)

Syntax
if (*boolean-expression*)
    statement;

[else
    statement;
]

Description

The **if** reserved word is used to build a conditional statement that may be used if the **boolean expression** is a "true" value. The statement is executed only if the **boolean expression** resolves to a "true" result. If the **boolean expression** is "false" and an else clause is present (following the statement), the else statement is executed.

Examples

```
// Check to see whether the number of students in the course is equal to 25.
// If so, close this section by setting the classFull flag to "true".
if (numberOfStudents == 25)
    classFull = true;
```

```
// If the user-entered value is the string "Java", then print the names of
// two other OOP languages.
if (enteredValue.equals ("Java")) {
    System.out.println ("Smalltalk");
    System.out.println ("C++");
}
```

Tips

- If the **boolean expression** does not resolve to a boolean result ("true" or "false"), a compile-time error is generated.

- To execute multiple statements when the **boolean expression** is a "true" value, enclose the statements to execute with braces, creating a statement block (see the second example).

- It is possible to nest **if** statements (the **if** reserved word, the **boolean expression**, and the statement). That is, an **if** statement can be executed as the result of another **if** statement.

See also

- bool (p. 13)
- false (p. 9)
- true (p. 9)

inline (modifier)

Syntax

[**inline**] *data-type function-name* ([*parameter-list*]) { ... }

Description

The **inline** reserved word is used to modify the definition of a function. By modifying a function to be **inline**, the compiler is permitted to replace a call to the function with a modified version of the body of the function.

This modification helps to speed up the execution of the code, since function calls add the overhead of additional memory being used (and then later released) as well as other managerial functionality which adds additional processing time.

Example

```
// Defines the inline function concatSuffix which appends the string
// " Thank you very much!" to the parameter string.
inline string concatSuffix (string base) {
    return base + " Thank you very much!";
}

int main ( ) {
    // Output the result of the concatSuffix function, modifying the
    // string literal it is passed.  Since the function is inline, the body of
    // the function (with modifications to deal with the parameter) will replace
    // the call to the function below.
    cout << concatSuffix ("I appreciate your time in this matter.") << endl;

    return 0;
}
```

Tips

- **Inline** functions are most often defined in header files due to the fact that an **inline** function needs to be defined in each file in which it is called.

- The decision to include the **inline** function's body at the point of the call is ultimately left to the compiler.

- The use of **inline** functions is a tradeoff, speed for the complexity of the rewriting and insertion of the function body. Thus, **inline** functions tend to be rather small – usually only several lines in length to keep the rewriting to a minimum.

See also

None.

int (data type)

Syntax

[modifier] **int** *variable-name* [= *initial-value-expression*];

Description

The reserved word **int** is used to declare one or more variables of the integer data type.

Examples

```
// Declares an integer variable named alpha and sets its initial value to 19.
int alpha = 19;
```

```
// Declares two integer variables, beta and gamma, and sets gamma's
// initial value to -5.
int beta, gamma = -5;
```

Tips

- When declaring an integer variable, you can optionally set the initial value of the variable by following the variable name with an equals sign and the initial value expression (as shown in brackets in the syntax statement).

- Multiple integer variables can be declared in the same statement by following each variable name with a comma (see the second example).

- As a function variable, **int**s should be initialized prior to use. If they are not, the variable will assume the value defined by the representation of its memory location. That is, the bits contained at the variable's true location in memory will be converted to a value of the variable's type (e.g. an **int**). Note that in this situation your compiler may provide a compile-time warning that the variable (when used) has not been previously initialized.

See also
None.

long (data type)

Syntax
[modifier] **long** *variable-name* [= *initial-value-expression*];

Description
The reserved word **long** is used to declare one or more variables of the **long** data type.

Examples

```
// Declares an integer variable named alpha and sets its initial value to 19.
long alpha = 19;
```

```
// Declares two integer variables, beta and gamma, and sets gamma's initial
```

```
// value to -55063L.
long beta, gamma = -55063L;
```

Tips

- When declaring a **long** variable, you can optionally set the initial value of the variable by following the **variable name** with an equals sign and the **initial value expression** (as shown in brackets in the syntax statement).

- Multiple **long** variables can be declared in the same statement by following each variable name with a comma (see the second example).

- As a function variable, **long**s should be initialized prior to use. If they are not, the variable will assume the value defined by the representation of its memory location. That is, the bits contained at the variable's true location in memory will be converted to a value of the variable's type (e.g. a **long**). Note that in this situation your compiler may provide a compile-time warning that the variable (when used) has not been previously initialized.

- To reduce the confusion between ints, **long**s, and other data types which store integer data, it is customary to append either the 'l' or the 'L' character when specifying a literal **long** value. This often occurs when initializing **long** variables. (See the examples above.)

See also
None.

mutable (modifier)

Syntax
[**mutable**] *data-type variable-name* [= *initial-value-expression*] ;

Description
The **mutable** modifier can be used to permit an instance variable (data member) from a constant object to be modified. The altering of this value is performed by assignment in a constant member function in the object. Without the **mutable** reserved word, the instance variable contained in the constant object would not be able to be modified.

Example

```
// Represents a school's sporting team
class Team {
private:
    string teamName;    // holds the team's name
    mutable int wins;    // holds the number of wins for the team
    mutable int losses; // stores the number of losses for the team
```

```
public:
    // Constructor for the Team object, sets name and wins/losses to zero
    Team (string name ) {
        this->teamName = name;
        this->wins = 0;
        this->losses = 0;
    }

    // Function that increases the number of wins
    void addWin ( ) const {
        this->wins++;
    }

    // Function that increases the number of losses
    void addLoss ( ) const {
        this->losses++;
    }
};

int main ( ) {
    // Create a constant Team object and then modify one of its
    // constant data fields via a call to addWin
    const Team nova ("Villanova Wildcats");
    nova.addWin ( );

    return 0;
}
```

Tips
- The mutable data member (instance variable) may only be modified through the body of a const member function.

See also
- const (p. 21)

namespace (definition)

Syntax

namespace *namespace-name* {
    // variables, functions, and classes defined here are part of this namespace

    ...

}

Description

The **namespace** reserved word is used to define a block of variables, functions, and/or classes as part of a specified abstract region of code. Members contained in this **namespace** will not conflict with other similarly named members from other namespaces.

Example

```
namespace tcnj {
    class department {
    private:
        string nameOfChair; // stores the name of the department chair
        int ageofDept; // stores the age of this department (in years)
        int numOfFaculty; // stores the number of faculty in this department

    public:
        // Returns the number of faculty from this deparment
        int getNumOfFaculty ( ) {
            return numOfFaculty;
        }
    };
}
```

Tips

* **Namespace**s are particularly helpful in a project that requires a large amount of source code. Multiple developers can each create and define their own classes, functions, and variables in their own **namespace**s without concern for naming conflicts (where two or more classes have the same name).
* You can insert variables, functions, and classes into a **namespace** that you define.
* If you don't wish to put all of your **namespace**'s contents in one file, you can define other **namespace** blocks (each with the same **namespace** name) in other source code files.
* Members of the **namespace** can be accessed outside the body of the **namespace** through the use of the reserved word.

See also

* using (p. 63)

new (operator)

Syntax

[variable-type*] variable-name = **new** data-type-name [(parameter-list)];

or

[variable-type*] variable-name = **new** *data-type-name [array-size]*;

Description

The **new** reserved word is used to create a **new** object (instance) of the specified **data type**. In the first syntax example, the allocation of the requested **data type** can be followed by an optional call to the **data type**'s constructor passing it any necessary parameters. In the second syntax example, the allocation creates an array of the specified **data type**. Both examples set a pointer to the newly created object or array to the specified pointer.

Examples

```
// Creates a new Student pointer named freshman and then creates the Student
// object by calling its default constructor.
Student* freshman;
freshman = new Student;
```

```
// Creates a new Student pointer named gradStudent with the specified name
// and age.
Student* gradStudent = new Student ("Michelle", 38);
```

```
// Creates an array of 50 integers and sets the grades pointer to the base address
// of the array.  The loop that follows the declaration and initialization of the
// pointer sets the initial values of each cell of the array.
int* grades = new int[50];
for (int i=0; i<50; i++)
    grades[i] = 0;
```

Tips

- Variables created at run-time are also known as dynamic data.
- Dynamic data variables which are created using the **new** operator should be destroyed when they are no longer needed. Destruction occurs through the use of the delete operator.

See also
- delete (p. 24)

operator (definition)

Syntax

return_type **operator** *op_symbol* (*parameters*) { ... }

or

return_type class_name::**operator** *op_symbol* (*parameters*) { … }

Description

The **operator** reserved word is used to define a function named operator which defines an overloaded operator (defined by the *op_symbol*). By creating such a function, an operator can be overloaded to provide a mechanism to apply existing operators to manipulate class objects.

Examples

```
// Defines a simple overloaded difference operator that returns the difference
// of two Shoe objects
int operator-(Shoe& yours, Shoe& mine) {
    return abs (yours.getSize ( ) - mine.getSize ( ));
}
```

```
class Boot {
...

public:
...

    // Overloading the plus operator to permit resizing of this boot by
    // the specified size.
    int operator+(int biggerSize) {
        this->size += biggerSize;
        return this->size;
    }
};

int main ( ) {
    // Defines two Shoe objects, each with initial values.  Then, prints the
    // difference between the objects, as defined by the Shoe class' operator
    // function "-".
    Shoe alpha (10);
    Shoe beta (7);
    cout << alpha-beta << endl;

    // Defines a single Boot object.  Then, the result of calling the Boot's "+"
    // operator function.
    Boot gamma (12);
    cout << gamma+(4) << endl;

    return 0;
}
```

Tips
- You cannot overload the following operators: sizeof, typeid, ?:, ::, ., and .*
- Nearly all of the other operators in C++ can be overloaded. This includes, but is not limited to: '!', '*', '/', '+', '-', '&', '%', '=', '<', '<<', '>', '>>', and many others.

See also
None.

private (qualifier)

Syntax

private:
> *member-data-and / or-functions;*

or

class *class-name* [: [**protected**] *class-name-to-extend* [, *class-name-to-extend*]] {
> // Class members (variables and functions) are defined here.
};

Description
The **private** reserved word is used to declare those members of a class (constants, variables, functions, and data types) which are accessible only to the functions contained in the same class.

Example

```
class Team {
private:
    string sport; // Stores the name of the sport this team plays
    string name; // Stores the name of this team
    int numPlayers; // Holds the number of current players on this team
    int numCoaches; // Holds the number of coaches associated with this team
    int recordThisSeason; // Holds the current record (winning %) of this team

public:
    // Returns the name of the sport this team plays
    string getSport ( ) {
        return sport;
    }

    // Sets the name of this team to the value specified.
    void setName (string teamName) {
```

```
        name = teamName;
    }
};
```

Tip

- The use of **private** members helps to promote encapsulation of a class. The application of this modifier to a class member is an integral decision of the engineering of software.

- When the **private** reserved word is used to assign an inheritance access level (see the second syntax form above), protected and public members in the base class are **private** in the derived class.

See also

- protected (p. 44)   • public (p. 45)

---

protected (qualifier)

Syntax

protected:

    member-data-and / or-functions;

or

class *class-name* [: [**protected**] *class-name-to-extend* [, *class-name-to-extend*]] {
    // Class members (variables and functions) are defined here.
};

Description

The **protected** reserved word is used to declare those members of a class (constants, variables, functions, and data types) which are accessible only to the functions contained in the same class and derived classes.

Example

```
class Team {
protected:
    string sport; // Stores the name of the sport this team plays
    string name; // Stores the name of this team
    int numPlayers; // Holds the number of current players on this team
    int numCoaches; // Holds the number of coaches associated with this team
    int recordThisSeason; // Holds the current record (winning %) of this team

public:
    // Returns the name of the sport this team plays
```

```
string getSport ( ) {
    return sport;
}

// Sets the name of this team to the value specified.
void setName (string teamName) {
    name = teamName;
}
};
```

Tips

- The use of **protected** members helps to promote encapsulation of a class. The application of this modifier to a class member is an integral decision of the engineering of software.

- When the **protected** reserved word is used to assign an inheritance access level (see the second syntax form above), **protected** and public members in the base class are protected in the derived class.

See also

- private (p. 43)
- public (p. 45)

public (qualifier)

Syntax

public:

> *member-data-and / or-functions;*

or

class *class-name* [: [**public**] *class-name-to-extend* [, *class-name-to-extend*]] {
> // Class members (variables and functions) are defined here.
};

Description

The **public** reserved word is used to declare those members of a class (constants, variables, functions, and data types) which are accessible anywhere in the program (including outside the defining class).

Public functions are generally used to provide a service (e.g., accessors and mutators) to other classes. **Public** data fields are generally considered poor programming (unless they are also declared as constants) because **public** data violate the notion of encapsulation of data within the encompassing class.

Example

```
class Rectangle {
public:
    // The static area function returns the area of a circle, given a radius. It
    // uses the defined PI value.
    static double area (double width, double height) {
        return width * height;
    }

    // The value of numSides is available to this and other classes but
    // cannot be changed.
    static const int SIDES = 4;
};
```

Tips

- If the start of the definition of a class contains no access modifier (private, protected, **public**), then the class members of that region are **public** by default.
- When the **public** reserved word is used to assign an inheritance access level (see the second syntax form above), public members in the base class remain **public** in the derived class, and protected members in the base class remain protected in the derived class.

See also

- private (p. 43)
- protected (p. 44)

register (modifier)

Syntax

[**register**] *data-type variable-name* [= *intial-value-expression*];

Description

By using the **register** reserved word when defining a variable, a request is issued to the compiler that the variable defined is stored in a machine register for faster access.

Example

```
int main ( ) {
    // Creates a Product object and requests that it is stored in a register
    // for easy and fast access.  A string version of the Product is then printed
    // by calling the accessor functions.
    register Product bodySpray ("Trenton Breeze", 15.50);
    cout << bodySpray.getName ( ) << ": $" << bodySpray.getPrice ( ) << endl;
```

```
    return 0;
}
```

Tips

- The **register** modifier is only a request to the compiler. The compiler may choose to ignore the request.

See also
None.

return (control)

Syntax
return [*expression*];

Description
The **return** reserved word is used alone or with the optional expression to create a statement used to **return** execution to the calling function. When encountered, execution ceases in the current function and execution is transferred to the statement in the calling function or constructor.

Examples

```
// The getPostalCode function returns the postal code value (an integer)
int getPostalCode ( ) {
    return postalCode;
}
```

```
// The setPostalCode function sets the postal code to the value specified
// and does not return a value.
void setPostalCode (int value) {
    postalCode = value;
    return;
}
```

Tips

- If an expression is present in a **return** statement, the expression's resulting data type must match the data type specified to be returned according to the function's signature. That is, the expression must match the function's **return** type.
- Although it is possible to have multiple **return** statements, it is considered good programming practice to limit functions to containing one **return** statement.

- If a function does not **return** any data (the **return** type is void), a **return** statement need not be present. In the second example, it is present but returns nothing, so its presence does not cause any warnings or errors.

- Constructors can contain a **return** statement; but they must be devoid of the optional expression.

See also
- void (p. 66)

---

short (data type)

Syntax
[modifier] **short** *variable-name* [= *initial-value-expression*];

Description
The reserved word **short** is used to declare one or more variables of the **short** data type.

Examples

```
// Declares a short variable named alpha and sets its initial value to 19.
short alpha = 19;
```

```
// Declares two short variables, beta and gamma, and sets gamma's initial
// value to -5.
short beta, gamma = -5;
```

Tips
- When declaring a **short** variable, you can optionally set the initial value of the variable by following the variable name with an equals sign and the initial value expression (as shown in brackets in the syntax statement).

- Multiple **short** variables can be declared in the same statement by following each variable name with a comma (see the second example).

- As a function variable, **short**s should be initialized prior to use. If they are not, the variable will assume the value defined by the representation of its memory location. That is, the bits contained at the variable's true location in memory will be converted to a value of the variable's type (e.g. a **short**). Note that in this situation your compiler may provide a compile-time warning that the variable (when used) has not been previously initialized.

See also
None.

signed (modifier)

Syntax

[**signed**] *data-type variable-name* [*initial-value-expression*];

Description

The **signed** modifier may be applied to the declaration of an integer variable to modify the values that it can store. By applying the **signed** reserved word, the variable will store positive and negative integer values. Here, the variable's sign bit is used to store the sign of the stored value. Thus, the maximum value a **signed** variable can store will be less than the maximum value of an unsigned variable of the same type.

Example

```
signed short classEnrollement = 15;
signed int totalNumberOfStudents = 254333;
```

Tips

- The **signed** reserved word may only be applied to variables whose type is short, int, or long.
- If a variable is not modified as either **signed** or unsigned, then the variable defaults to a **signed** variable.

See also

- int (p. 36)
- long (p. 37)
- short (p. 49)
- signed (p. 49)

sizeof (operator)

Syntax

sizeof *expression*

or

sizeof (*data-type-name*)

Description

The **sizeof** operator returns the size in bytes of the named data type or the result of the specified expression.

Examples

```
// Define a short variable named shrtVar and intialize it to zero.
short shrtVar = 0;
```

```
// Print out the size of the short data type for this system.
cout << "A short is " << sizeof shrtVar << " bytes." << endl;
```

```
// Print out the size of the short data type for this system.
cout << "A long is " << sizeof (long) << " bytes." << endl;
```

Tips

- The expression used in the first syntax option (shown above) can be a simple variable name or a more complex expression to evaluate. In either case, the expression is fully evaluated and then the resulting size is calculated.

- The **sizeof** operator returns a value of type size_t. On most platforms this is the equivalent of an unsigned integer value.

See also
None.

static (modifier)

Syntax

[**static**] *data-type function-name* ([*parameter-declarations*]) { ... }

or

[**static**] *data-type variable-name* [= *initial-value*];

Description

The **static** reserved word is used to modify a function or data variable to be a class function (or data variable) rather than an instance function (or data variable). That is, there will only be one copy of the function or data variable for all objects of the class that contains it.

Examples

```
void setUpProgram ( ) {
    static string schoolName = "TCNJ";
    static const int areaCode = 609;
}
```

```
class Course {
private:
    // The static crsPrefix identifier is used in printing the course prefix.
    static const int crsPrefix = 2005;
```

```
public:
    // The getPrefix function returns the static data crsPrefix
    static int getPrefix ( ) {
        return crsPrefix;
    }
};
```

Tips

- A **static** function can reference only **static** data and other **static** functions—it has no knowledge of instances of the class that contains it. All instances of a class can access instance data and instance functions as well as the **static** data and **static** functions of the class.

- If a **static** variable's value is modified, the change is seen by all of the instances of a class.

- Constant data fields (declared with the const reserved word) are often modified with the **static** reserved word to preserve memory. (Multiple copies of a value that cannot be changed are wasteful.)

See also

None.

struct (user–defined data type)

Syntax

struct *data-type-name* {
    // Member data variables are declared here

    ...
};

Description

The **struct** reserved word is used to create user-defined data types which encompass other data. A **struct** in C++ is very similar to a class; however, data members in a C++ **struct** are publically accessible and there are no functions in the structure.

Example

```
// Defines a simple structure to represent an address (of a building, house, etc.)
struct Address {
    int number;  // Stores the street number
    string street;  // Stores the street name
    string city;  // Stores the city name
    string stateZip;  // Stores the state and zip code as one string
```

```
};

// Creates a shippingAddress variable and populates it with data
Address shippingAddr;
shippingAddr.number = 55;
shippingAddr.street = "Adams Drive";
shippingAddr.city = "Portsmouth";
shippingAddr.stateZip = "RI02871";
```

Tips

- To access a data member of a **struct**, use the **struct** variable's name, followed by a period character, followed by the member variable's name. See the example above.

- A **struct**'s declaration ends in a semicolon, as does a class declaration.

See also
None.

switch (control)

Syntax
```
switch ( expression ) {
    // One or more case clauses of the form
    [ case constant-expression:
        statement(s);
        [ break; ]
    ]

    [ default:
        statement(s);
        [ break; ]
    ]
}
```

Description
The **switch** statement is used to provide an option for selecting and executing one of a number of paths. The selection is based on the result of the **expression** and the **switch** statement containing a case label for the path that matches the **expression**'s result.

Examples

```
char letter = 'i';
string characterType = "unknown";
```

```
// Switch on the letter variable.
switch (letter) {
    // if 'letter' is 'a', 'e', 'i', 'o', or 'u' set the type to "vowel"
    case 'a':
    case 'e':
    case 'i':
    case 'o':
    case 'u':
        characterType = "vowel";
        break;

    // Otherwise, set the type to consonant.
    default:
        characterType = "consonant";
        break;
}
```

```
int value = 3;

// Switch on the value variable.
switch (value) {
    // If value is 1, increment by one.
    case 1:
        value++;
        break;

    // If value is 3, increment by two.
    case 3:
        value += 2;
        break;
}
```

Tips

- The **switch** expression must evaluate to a bool, char, int, long, or short value.
- Any statement within the **switch** statement block must be labeled by a case or default label.

See also
- break (p. 14)
- case (p. 15)
- default (p. 23)

template (modifier/class-related)

Syntax

template <typename *data-type* [, typename/class *data-type/class-name*] >
class *class-name* { ... }

or

template <class class-name [, typename/class *data-type/class-name*] >
class *class-name* { ... }

or

template <typename T>
return-type function-name ([*parameter-list*]){ ... }

or

template <class T>
return-type function-name ([*parameter-list*]){ ... }

Description

The **template** reserved word is used to create **template** classes and functions. These types of classes and functions are considered general purpose in nature and and provide the ability to provide type parameterization to the definition of a class or function.

Examples

```
// Defines a class named Node which can contain an integer nodeNumber and
// an array of the template type specified when the class is instantiated.
template <typename T>
class Node {
private:
    int nodeNumber;  // stores the node's (unique) number
    T storageCells[10]; // stores up to 10 items of type T

    // Remainder of class goes here
};

void templateTester ( ) {
    // Define the integerNodes variable of type Node<int>, which is a
    // templated class that stores/operates on ints (in this example)
    Node<int> integerNodes;

    // Remainder of function goes here
}
```

```cpp
// The calculateAverage function calculates the average of the contents of
// the array the function is passed.  It uses template to support a wider
// variety of data types in the array (shorts, ints, floats, etc.)
template <typename T>
T calculateAverage (T data[], int size) {
    T sum = 0, count = 0;

    for (int index = 0; index < size; index++) {
        count++;
        sum += data[index];
    }
    return sum / count;
}

int main () {
    // Define two arrays of quiz and project grades of differing data-types
    int quizGrades[] = {75, 67, 100, 99, 82, 88};
    float projectGrades[] = {90.5f, 100.0f, 77.6f, 84.5f};

    // Calculate and print the average of each array
    cout << "Quiz average: " << calculateAverage (quizGrades, 6) << endl;
    cout << "Project average: " << calculateAverage (projectGrades, 4) << endl;

    return 0;
}
```

Tips

- **Template**s can be most helpful when attempting to author source code that operates identically on different data types.
- The parameters for a C++ template can include one or more types or classes. When building the **template** parameter list, use the typename reserved word to add data types and the class reserved word to add class parameters.
- The templating of a class or function occurs at compile time.

See also

- typename (p. 60)

this (class–related)

Syntax

this->data-field

or

this.function-name ([parameter-list]);

Description

The **this** reserved word in C++ is a pointer (within an object) to refer to itself. It is most often used in constructors and instance functions to refer to instance data fields that may have the same name as the formal parameters of the constructor or function. The **this** pointer can therefore be used to clarify which variable (the formal parameter or instance data field) you wish to reference.

Example

```
class Section {
private:
    // The instance variables sectionNumber and sectionEnrollment keep track of
    // key information about each instance of a course's section.
    int sectionNumber;
    int sectionEnrollment;

public:
    // The Section constructor accepts values for the section number and
    // the size of this section.
    Section (int sectionNumber, int sectionEnrollment) {
        this->sectionNumber = sectionNumber;
        this->sectionEnrollment = sectionEnrollment;
    }
};
```

Tip

- The **this** reserved word is a pointer to the current object. It can also be used as a parameter to a function. For example, enrollment.add (**this**);
- A pointer to the current object can be returned from a function by a statement such as return *****this**;

See also

None.

throw (control)

Syntax
throw *expression*;

Description

The **throw** reserved word is used to cause a primitive value or object to be thrown as an exception. Thrown exceptions that are not caught by a catch block propagate upward through the calling function(s) until they are caught. If the exception propogates backward through all previous calling functions and is not caught, the program will terminate.

Example

```
void scoreChecker (int score) {
    try {
        if (score < 75)
            throw LowScoreException ("A low score has been discovered!");
    }
    catch (LowScoreException& lse) {
        cout << "Warning: " << lse.getException ( ) << endl;
    }
}
```

Tips
- The expression type in the **throw** statement can be a primitive value or an object.
- Strings and enumerated types can be thrown, but generally speaking the throwing (and subsequent catching) of objects is considered to be easier and less problematic.
- The throwing of primitive data types is considered a bad programming habit and may lead to ambiguous errors.

See also
- catch (p. 17)

try (control)

Syntax
try {
    statement(s);
}

```
catch (data-type variable-name) {
    statement(s);
}
```

Description

The **try** reserved word is part of the larger **try**/catch statement. Each of these reserved words encloses a block of one or more statements that are executed under certain circumstances. The **try** block is executed first, until it completes execution of its statements or an exception is thrown.

If an exception arises, each catch clause is examined one at a time, in linear order, to determine whether the thrown exception matches a particular **exception type**. A match is made if the type of the exception thrown can be assigned to the type being caught. If a match does occur, the statement(s) in the matching catch clause are executed. If an exception does not arise while executing the **try** block, processing continues following the last catch block.

Example

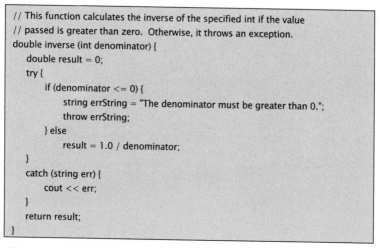

```
// This function calculates the inverse of the specified int if the value
// passed is greater than zero. Otherwise, it throws an exception.
double inverse (int denominator) {
    double result = 0;
    try {
        if (denominator <= 0) {
            string errString = "The denominator must be greater than 0.";
            throw errString;
        } else
            result = 1.0 / denominator;
    }
    catch (string err) {
        cout << err;
    }
    return result;
}
```

Tips

- A **try** block can have zero or more catch clauses associated with it as long as a different type of exception is being caught by each clause.

See also

- catch (p. 17)
- throw (p. 57)

typedef (statement)

Syntax
typedef *old-type-name new-type-name*;

Description
The **typedef** statement is used to define a new type name (alias) based upon an existing type name. Generally, this style of replacement is used when the old type name is overly long and an alias is more convenient to the readability of the program.

Examples

```cpp
// Redefine the unsigned int data type to one named distance
typedef unsigned int distance;

// Declare two distance variables for use below
distance length=0, width=0;

cout << "Enter the length in inches: ";
cin >> length;

cout << "Enter the width in inches: ";
cin >> width;
```

```cpp
typedef struct {
    string name;
    int age;
    string phoneNum;
} classmate;
```

Tips
- The **typedef** statment can also be combined with the struct reserved word to create a new data type that is a user-defined structure type (see the second example above).
- Renaming (or aliasing) a data type's name in no way changes the functionality of the data type.

See also
- struct (p. 51)

typeid (operator)

Syntax

typeid (*expression*)

or

typeid (*class-name*)

Description

The **typeid** operator evaluates a given expression or class-name and returns a reference to a type_info object (defined in typeinfo.h). The type_info object will contain relevant information about the true type of the expression or class specified.

Example

```
class Employee {
...
};

class FullTime : public Employee {
...
};

int main ( ) {
    // Instantiate both a FullTime object and an Employee object
    FullTime* ftEmp = new FullTime;
    Employee* emp = ftEmp;

    // Obtain the type each reference, despite the type of the underlying object
    cout << typeid (emp).name ( ) << endl;
    cout << typeid (ftEmp).name ( ) << endl;

    return 0;
}
```

Tips

• The class-name or expression result from the **typeid** operator can be accessed through the name function in the type_info object.

See also

None.

typename (modifier)

Syntax

template < **typename** *data-type* [, **typename** *data-type*] >
class *class-name* { … }

or

template <**typename** T>
return-type function-name ([*parameter-list*]){ … }

Description

The **typename** reserved word is used to signify that an unknown template parameter identifier is a type (rather than a value).

Example

```
// The calculateAverage function calculates the average of the contents of
// the array the function is passed.  It uses template to support a wider
// variety of data types in the array (shorts, ints, floats, etc.)
template <typename T>
T calculateAverage (T data[ ], int size) {
   T sum = 0, count = 0;

   for (int index = 0; index < size; index++) {
       count++;
       sum += data[index];
   }
   return sum / count;
}
```

Tips

• The **typename** reserved word can be used in place of the class reserved word when defining template parameters.

See also

• template (p. 54)

---

union (user-defined data type)

Syntax

union *data-type-name* {
    // Member data variables are declared here

    …

};

Description

Unions are user-defined data structures which can hold a single data member at a time. However, in defining a union, multiple data members are often specified. Thus, at any given time, a union variable may represent one of the specified data members.

Example

```
int main ( ) {
    // Defines an exaple union
    union exampleUnion {
        int alpha;
        char beta;
        float delta;
    };

    // Creates an exampleUnion variable and populates it with int data
    exampleUnion unionTester;
    unionTester.alpha = 2005;
    cout << unionTester.alpha << endl;

    // Overwrites the int data above and inserts character data
    unionTester.beta = 'P';
    cout << unionTester.beta << endl;

    return 0;
}
```

Tips

- A **union** will utilize as much memory space as its largest member's size.
- A **union** cannot contain member objects which define constructors or destructors.
- **Union**s can be nested inside the definition of a struct.

See also

- struct (p. 51)

unsigned (modifier)

Syntax

[**unsigned**] *data-type variable-name* [*initial-value-expression*];

Description

The **unsigned** modifier may be applied to the declaration of an integer variable to modify the values that it can store. By applying the **unsigned** reserved word, the variable will store only values of zero or greater. Additionally, the sign bit (used to store the sign of a value in signed variables) will be used in the value's representation. Thus, the maximum value an **unsigned** variable can store will be greater than the maximum value of a signed variable of the same type.

Example

```
unsigned short classEnrollement = 15u;
unsigned int totalNumberOfStudents = 254333U;
```

Tips

* The **unsigned** reserved word may only be applied to variables whose type is short, int, or long.

* A literal constant value which is an **unsigned** int must end in a 'U' or 'u' character.

* If a negative value is assigned to an **unsigned** variable, the resulting assigned value will not be negative, but a larger, positive value (which is usually unexpected).

* If a variable is not modified as either signed or **unsigned**, then the variable defaults to a signed variable.

See also

* int (p. 36)
* long (p. 37)

* short (p. 49)
* signed (p. 49)

using (directive)

Syntax

using namespace *namespace-name*;

Description

The **using** directive specifies that names in the specified namespace can be referenced without an explicit qualifier. That is, by applying the **using** directive to a given namespace all of the names within that space may be referenced without qualifying which namespace they are drawn from.

Example

```
#include <string>
#include <iomanip>
using namespace std;

class Products {
```

```
...
}
```

Tips

- To permit the use of just one name in a namespace, use a **using** declaration to provide just the single name. E.g. **using** std::cout

See also

- namespace (p. 39)

virtual (modifier)

Syntax

[**virtual**] *return_type function_name* ([*parameter-list*]);

or

[**virtual**] *return_type function_name* ([*parameter-list*]) { ... }

or

virtual *return_type function_name* ([*parameter-list*]) = 0;

Description

The **virtual** modifier creates a function definition which is dynamically bound at run time. The defined function is overridden in derived classes.

In the second syntax form above, the member function is declared with no definition. Thus, it is considered to be an abstract function. In this situation, a derived class must override the function or the derived class will be abstract.

Example

```cpp
class Shape {
protected:
    int width;  // Stores the width of this shape
    int height; // Stores the height of this shape

public:
    // The virtual function getArea calculates and returns the area of
    // a square shape,
    virtual double area ( ) {
        return height * width;
    }

    // The constructor for the Shape class.  A square is assumed.
```

```
    Shape (int size) {
        this->width = size;
        this->height = size;
    }
};

class Triangle: public Shape {
public:
    // The constructor for the Triangle class, calls the base class' constructor
    Triangle (int a, int b)
        :Shape (a)
    {
        this->height = b;
    }

    // Returns the area for this triangle (a right triangle is assumed)
    double area ( ) {
        return height * width / 2.0;
    }
};

// Dispatches the call to obtain the area for shape specified by the pointer.
// The call to area will call the appropriate version of the function area,
// depending on the actual type that 's' points to.
double getArea (Shape& s) {
    return s.area ( );
}

int main ( ) {
    // Set up two objects of the base class and derived class.
    Shape baseShape (5);
    Triangle triangleShape (10, 10);

    // Print the objects' areas.   The exact area calcuation depends on
    // what is actually passed to the getArea function.
    cout << "Area of shape: " << getArea (baseShape) << endl;
    cout << "Area of square: " << getArea (triangleShape) << endl;

    return 0;
}
```

Tips

- The **virtual** reserved word is only used when the function is first defined (base class), not overridden (child classes).

- When overriding a **virtual** function in a derived class, the signature of the function (*return_type*, *function_name*, and *parameter-list*) must be the same as the function definition in the base class.

- Only non-static class member functions can have a **virtual** modifier applied.

See also
None.

---

void (data type)

Syntax
void *function-name* ([*parameter-declarations*]) { ... }

Description
The **void** reserved word is used to denote the absence of a data value to be returned at the conclusion of a function's execution.

Example

```
// The setAge function sets the age to the value of the myAge parameter,
// but returns nothing to the calling function.
void setAge (int myAge) {
    age = myAge;
}
```

Tips

- If you use the **void** reserved word in the declaration of a function, be sure that the function lacks a return statement or the return statement (if used) lacks a value to return. The **void** reserved word prevents returning a value to the calling function.

- If you wish to return a value at the conclusion of a function's execution, use the return reserved word (see page 47) and modify the function's signature to include the proper return type.

See also
- return (p. 47)

volatile (modifier)

Syntax

[**volatile**] *data-type variable-name* [= *initial-value-expression*];

or

[**volatile**] *return-type function-name* ([*parameter-list*]);

Description

The **volatile** reserved word is used to modify a local or instance variable's declaration to indicate that its contents are highly subject to change by another process (thread), the hardware, or the operating system. If modified as **volatile**, the compiler is instructed not to attempt to optimize instructions that access the variable. Thus, the variable is always read (where an optimization might use a previous read to obtain the value) to ensure the correct value is obtained.

Example

```
// The WorkshopSection class contains enrollment and naming information about
// each workshop offered. Note that the currentEnrollment instance field is
// highly subject to change via threads handling workshop enrollment processing.
// Thus it is a volatile instance field.
class WorkshopSection {
private:
    volatile int currentEnrollment;
    string courseName;
    const static int maxSize = 24;
...
};
```

Tip

• The **volatile** reserved word is generally only used in advanced (complex) programs. As an introductory student, you are not likely to encounter an opportunity to use **volatile** modifier.

See also
None.

while (control)

Syntax
while (*boolean-expression*)
    statement;

Description

The **while** loop repeats the statement (or statements, if enclosed in braces) until the **boolean expression** evaluates to a "false" result. Because of its structure, the statement is not guaranteed to be executed at all. If the expression is "false" the first time it is analyzed, the statement will never be executed. The **boolean expression** that controls the loop is evaluated before executing the statement portion (body) of the loop.

Examples

```
// Loop until alpha is no longer less than the target; increase alpha by two
// each time through the loop.
while (alpha < target)
    alpha = alpha + 2;
```

```
// Loop while alpha is less than the target and beta is greater than five.
// The body of the loop modifies the values of the alpha and beta variables.
while (alpha < target && beta > 5) {
    alpha++;
    beta = beta - 1;
}
```

Tips

- The statement portion of the **while** loop is not guaranteed to execute at all. Execution depends on the result of the **boolean expression**.

- If the **boolean expression** does not resolve to a boolean result ("true" or "false"), a compile-time error is generated.

- To execute multiple statements as the body of the **while** loop, enclose the statements to execute in braces, creating a statement block (see the second example).

- Be sure that the **boolean expression** changes as part of the body of the loop. If the value of the expression does not change, the loop will be performed endlessly. This situation is known as an *endless loop*.

- Keep in mind that the **boolean expression** can comprise multiple boolean expressions joined by logical operators.

- A **while** loop may contain other loops (do, for, **while**), thereby creating *nested loops*.

- Break and continue statements can be used in **while** loops.

See also

- break (p. 14)
- continue (p. 22)
- do (p. 25)
- false (p. 9)
- for (p. 30)
- true (p. 9)

Commonly Used C++ Header Files and Their Contents

Notes

- Some compilers will automatically import useful C lanauge header files as part of the C++ header files. Generally speaking, this occurs when a C++ header file permits the exposure of defined constants. We have included the C++ header file listings below, however with the name of the C header file indicated (see the defined constants list in the cfloat header file as an example). Not all compilers support this behavior and thus, you may need to include the corresponding C header file to obtain access to the constants. Refer to your compiler's documentation to determine how to proceed.

- Some of the functions listed below include a data type named size_t. For all intents and purposes, the size_t can be treated as an int value when listed as a function parameter or return type.

<cassert>

Description

The cassert header file contains the support for the assert function. With assert, you can terminate execution of a program if a run-time expression is true (non-zero result). Termination results in the printing of an error message to the console.

Defined Constants
None.

Defined Functions
void assert (int)

<cctype>

Description

The cctype header file contains a variety of functions for verifying the status of a character value. For example, a single character value can be verified to be a lowercase character. For functions that return an integer value, a true (non-zero) or false (zero) value is returned. Functions that return a character value are conversion functions and are returning a modification of the parameter.

Defined Constants

None.

Defined Functions

int isalnum (char)
int isalpha (char)
int isdigit (char)
int isgraph (char)
int islower (char)
int isprint (char)
int ispunct (char)
int isspace (char)
int isupper (char)
char tolower (char)
char toupper (char)

<cfloat>

Description

The cfloat header file defines a variety of constant values which represent the minimum and maximum values of primitive floating point data types. Since the limits for each data type vary from platform to platform, values are not provided below. Check your documentation for more information regarding the primitive data types for your platform.

Defined Constants (defined in float.h)

DBL_DIG
DBL_EPSILON
DBL_MANT_DIG
DBL_MAX
DBL_MAX_10_EXP
DBL_MAX_EXP
DBL_MIN
DBL_MIN_10_EXP
DBL_MIN_EXP
FLT_DIG
FLT_EPSILON
FLT_MANT_DIG
FLT_MAX
FLT_MAX_10_EXP
FLT_MAX_EXP
FLT_MIN
FLT_MIN_10_EXP

FLT_MIN_EXP
FLT_RADIX
FLT_ROUNDS
LDBL_DIG
LDBL_EPSILON
LDBL_MANT_DIG
LDBL_MAX
LDBL_MAX_10_EXP
LDBL_MAX_EXP
LDBL_MIN
LDBL_MIN_10_EXP
LDBL_MIN_EXP

Defined Functions

None.

<climits>

Description

The climits header file defines a variety of constant values which represent the minimum and maximum values of primitive integer data types. Since the limits for each data type vary from platform to platform, values are not provided below. Check your documentation for more information regarding the primitive data types for your platform.

Defined Constants (defined in limits.h)

CHAR_BIT
CHAR_MAX
CHAR_MIN
INT_MAX
INT_MIN
LONG_MAX
LONG_MIN
MB_LEN_MAX
SCHAR_MAX
SCHAR_MIN
SHRT_MAX
SHRT_MIN
UCHAR_MAX
UINT_MAX
ULONG_MAX
USHRT_MAX

Defined Functions
    None.

<cmath>

Description

The cmath header file contains commonly used math functions to calculate such values as sine, cosine, tangent, and many others. Nearly all of the functions accept a single double value as a parameter (except for the power function) and return a double value as a result.

Defined Constants (defined in math.h)

M_E	2.7182818284590452354
M_LOG2E	1.4426950408889634074
M_LOG10E	0.43429448190325182765
M_LN2	0.69314718055994530942
M_LN10	2.30258509299404568402
M_PI	3.14159265358979323846
M_PI_2	1.57079632679489661923
M_PI_4	0.78539816339744830962
M_1_PI	0.31830988618379067154
M_2_PI	0.63661977236758134308
M_2_SQRTPI	1.12837916709551257390
M_SQRT2	1.41421356237309504880
M_SQRT1_2	0.70710678118654752440

Defined Functions

```
double acos (double)
double asin (double)
double atan (double)
double atan2 (double, double)
double ceil (double)
double cos (double)
double cosh (double)
double exp (double)
double fabs (double)
double floor (double)
double fmod (double, double)
double frexp (double, int *)
double ldexp (double, int)
double log (double)
double log10 (double)
double modf (double, double *)
double pow (double, double)
```

double sin (double)
double sinh (double)
double sqrt (double)
double tan (double)
double tanh (double)

<cstdlib>

Description

The cstdlib header file contains functions to support the calculation of the absolute value of various forms of integer values, memory allocation and deallocation, character conversion, and other miscellaneous functions.

Defined Constants

None significant.

Defined Functions

void abort (void)
int abs (int)
double atof (const char *)
int atoi (const char *)
long atol (const char *)
void *calloc (size_t)
void exit (int)
void free (void *)
long int labs (long int)
long long int llabs (long long int)
void *malloc (size_t)
int rand ( )
void realloc (void *, size_t)
int srand (int)
int system (const char *)

<cstring>

Description

The cstring header file contains a variety of functions which support string and memory manipulations. (Note, check that the memory functions are really accessible via only the including of the cstring header file. We may not wish to list them.)

Defined Constants

   None significant.

Defined Functions

```
char *strcat (char *, char *)
char *strncat (char *, char *, size_t)
int strcmp (char *, char *)
int strncmp (char *, char *, size_t)
char *strcpy (char *, char *)
char *strncpy (char *, char *, size_t)
int strlen (char *)
size_t strnlen (char *, size_t)
void *memcpy (void *, const void *, size_t)
void *memmove (void *, const void *, size_t)
void *memccpy (void *, const void *, int, size_t)
void *memset (void *, int , size_t ) ;
int memcmp (const void *, const void *, size_t)
void *memchr (const void *, int, size_t)
void *memrchr (const void *, int, size_t)
int strcoll (const char *, const char *)
size_t strxfrm (char *, const char *, size_t)
char *strdup (const char *)
char *strndup (const char *, size_t)
char *strchr (const char *, int)
char *strrchr (const char *, int)
size_t strcspn (const char *, const char *)
size_t strspn (const char *, const char *)
char *strpbrk (const char *, const char *)
char *strstr (const char *, const char *)
char *strtok (char *, const char *)
char *strtok_r (char *, const char *, char **)
void *memmem (const void *, size_t, const void *, size_t)
char *strerror (int);
char *strerror_r (int, char *, size_t);
void bcopy (const void *, void *, size_t)
void bzero (void *, size_t);
int bcmp (const void *, const void *, size_t)
char *index (const char *, int)
char *rindex (const char *, int)
int ffs (int)
int ffsl (long int)
int strcasecmp (const char *, const char *)
int strncasecmp (const char *, const char *, size_t)
char *strsep (char **, const char *)
```

```
int strverscmp (const char *, const char *)
char *stpcpy (char *, const char *)
char *stpncpy (char *, const char *, size_t)
char *strfry (char *)
void *memfrob (void *, size_t)
char *basename (const char *)  (may not be defined in .NET in this header file)
char *strsignal (int)
```

<iomanip>

Description
The iomanip header file provides a variety of input and output manipulators specifically designed to ease formatting requirements and control over the input and output streams. To modify the output stream, embed the modifier as part of the output stream as if you were printing a variable or function result (e.g. cout << setprecision (5);)

Defined Manipulators
```
dec
fixed
hex
oct
scientific
setbase (int)
setfill (char)
setiosflags (int)
setprecision (int)
setw (int)
```

<iostream>

Description
The iostream header file contains the definition of the standard stream objects. By default, most compilers will automatically import the istream header file (see next page).

Defined Constants
```
istream cin
ostream cout
ostream cerr
ostream clog
```

Defined Functions

None.

<istream>

Description

The istream header file contains the definition the istream, ostream, and ios classes.

Defined Constants

None.

Defined Functions

None.

Defined Classes and Their Functions and Flags

istream

bool istream::fail ( )

istream& istream::get (char &)

istream& istream::unget ( )

istream& istream::seekg (long)

istream& istream::seekg (long, int)

long istream::tellg ( )

ostream

ostream& ostream::seekp (long)

ostream& ostream::seekp (long, int)

long ostream::tellp ( )

ios

ios::beg

ios::cur

ios::dec

ios::end

ios::fixed

ios::hex

ios::internal

ios::left

ios::oct

ios::right

ios::scientific

ios::showbase

ios::showpoint

ios::uppercase

<fstream>

Description
The fstream header file contains the definition the ifstream, ofstream, and fstream classes.

Defined Constants
None.

Defined Functions
None.

Defined Classes and Their Functions and Flags
ifstream
    void close ( )
    bool isopen ( )
    void ifstream::open (const char *)
ofstream
    void ofstream::open (string)
fstream
    void fstream::open (string)

<string>

Description
The string header file contains the definition the string data type (a specialized data type based upon a basic_string template which handles character data), and a number of functions and operators which can manipulate strings. Only a subset of the defined functions appear below – there are too list here. Each function also has many variant forms, so check your documentation to determine what is available on your system.

Defined Constants
None.

Defined Functions
None.

Defined Classes and Their Functions and Operators
string
    string& append (string&)
    string& assign (string&)
    const_reference at (int)
    int capacity ( )
    void clear ( )

```
int compare (const string&)
int copy (char*, int, int)
bool empty ( )
string& erase ( )
int find (const string&, int)
string& insert (int, string&)
int length ( )
int max_size ( )
void push_back (char)
string& replace (int, int, const string&)
void resize (int)
int size ( )
int substr (int, int)
void swap (string&)
+
=
+=
!=
==
>
>=
<
<=
<<
>>
```

Index